101 Toughest
Interview Questions

. . . and Answers
that Win the Job!

Surrey
Community
Services

Rehabilitaton
Programs

101
TOUGHEST
INTERVIEW
QUESTIONS

...AND ANSWERS
THAT WIN THE JOB!

Daniel Porot
with Frances Bolles Haynes

Ten Speed Press
Berkeley, California

Copyright © 1999 by Daniel Porot

A Kirsty Melville Book

Ten Speed Press
P.O. Box 7123
Berkeley, California 94707
www.tenspeed.com

Distributed in Australia by Simon and Schuster Australia, in Canada by Ten Speed Press Canada, in New Zealand by Southern Publishers Group, in South Africa by Real Books, in Southeast Asia by Berkeley Books, and in the United Kingdom and Europe by Airlift Book Company.

Cover and book design by Lisa Patrizio

Library of Congress Cataloging-in-Publication Data on file with the publisher.

ISBN 1-58008-068-5

First printing, 1999
Printed in Singapore

4 5 6 7 8 9 10 — 04 03 02 01

Contents

Introduction

Surprise is a thing we enjoy and a thing we fear. The element of surprise is a powerful tool in almost every situation. When people are surprised, they often respond in a way they would not respond if they had taken time to prepare. All of us have probably experienced a situation in which we thought of what we should have said after the time to say it had passed.

In many situations, we don't have the chance to say what we really mean—but interviewing does *not* have to be one of them.

This book was written to eliminate the surprise factor in interviews. We can prepare for an interview ahead of time so we will be able to respond exactly as we had intended and impart exactly the information we had hoped to impart.

By becoming familiar with the tough questions found in this book and by practicing thoughtful, well-reasoned answers, job hunters can improve their performance in an interview and increase their chances of being hired.

When all candidates for a job are fairly similar, you may not get hired because another candidate is more qualified or fits into the company culture better, but you never have to lose your chance at a job again because you did not prepare adequately. All it takes is practice.

Like everything in life, interviewing for a job takes practice to do well. Even with natural talent, opera singers, actors, or major league pitchers must practice to perfect their craft. It is a rare person who can do something well without ever practicing.

Yet, in what can be one of the most crucial and future-shaping activities we undertake—interviewing for a job—we often proceed blindly and ill-prepared, if we prepare at all. It is easy to assume that the skills required to perform a job are the same skills necessary to interview well for a job. This can be a highly inaccurate and costly assumption to make. A person can be a highly skilled engineer or a superb marketing manager, but if she lacks the ability to convince an interviewer of this, she will likely lose the chance to get the kind of job for which she is best suited.

Interviewing well is more an art than a science. It requires special skills and an understanding of what information the interviewer must have to make a decision. It requires a plan and a strategy.

Interviewers must deal with certain questions and

underlying issues if they are to determine who they want to hire. Chapter 1 deals with this topic in depth. There are also certain strategies job hunters can employ to significantly increase their chance of being the person who gets hired. Refer to chapter 2 for an in-depth discussion of these strategies.

WHY DID WE CHOOSE THIS FORMAT?

It's simple. When job hunters understand that preparation for an interview is essential, the question becomes, "How do I best prepare myself?" With that in mind, we have listed the 101 toughest interview questions on convenient tear-out cards, with possible responses on the reverse side. The cards are easy to use. You can sort them, shuffle them, select some, set others aside, come back to specific ones, store them in your purse or pocket, place them in the corner of your bathroom mirror, etc.

You can also carry questions with you to an interview. If you have a few minutes to spare beforehand, look through your cards one more time. During the interview, you will feel comfortable knowing that you are prepared and the questions and your answers are close to you.

THERE ARE NO CORRECT ANSWERS, ONLY APPROPRIATE STRATEGIES

The purpose of these cards is to help you prepare for an interview and think about the best answer *you* can give to any question asked. These cards do not provide "canned" answers for you to memorize and "rattle off" to an interviewer without making them specific to you. The suggested answers are best used as jumping off points for you to think about your own experience and skills and formulate your own answers. As you look over the questions, we suggest you write out concrete examples from your work life and experience that support your response. Some of the answers given will not apply to you in certain cases, and you must never run the risk of answering a question in an interview without specific information and examples to support what you have said.

Instructions

HOW TO USE THIS BOOK

Each card has two sides: **a question side** with one tough question (or statement) asked in a typical interview and **an answer side** with suggested ideas for formulating answers or attitudes to adopt in your response. The best strategy is to use the answers as a guide for formulating your own responses. If a suggested answer applies to you or your experience, you may want to memorize it. The answers provided are intended to be guides for you to create the best answer to any question asked during an interview.

USING THE CARDS

Tear the cards from the book.

When using the cards by yourself:

Look through the cards (question side) and select those questions that you feel present the biggest problems you will face in an interview. Any question you dread being asked in an interview is a question you should take extra time in preparing an answer. Any question you fear being asked is a question you must deal with before you get to the interview.

For each question, write down (on a separate sheet of paper) an answer you feel you might give to an interviewer. After you have written an answer, flip the card over and read the suggested answers. Select the one you like best and see how it compares to your written answer. Choose the answer you feel is the best for you for each question and practice it until you are comfortable. When you come up with a new or different answer, it is wise to check with friends, relatives, present or past co-workers, people you trust—and know you well—to see how they respond to it and what feedback they might give you.

When using the cards with a partner:

1. Sit down and face each other.

2. Select the cards to use. Five to fifteen questions per person is a good way to start. Questions can be selected randomly, or each person may choose those questions they most need to practice and give them to their partner to ask.

3. Begin. Each person takes a turn at being the interviewer and the candidate.

You can ask or answer questions alternately, or one person can be the interviewer until all questions are asked and answered, and then the other person begins as interviewer.

Every time an effective answer is given, jot it down and memorize it for future use in an interview.

4. Once finished, review all the questions and the best answers. It is always a good strategy to double check with others who know you well (the more the better) to ensure each answer is the best possible one for you.

1
Understanding the Interviewer's Concerns

An interviewer must make hiring decisions. To do this, three basic issues must be covered in the questions they ask:

1. Can you actually do the job? Is your experience, training, education, aptitude, and interest sufficient so you will be productive for me?

2. Who are you? What are you like? What characteristics and traits do you possess?

3. Will you fit in with the others in my company/organization? Will you be part of a problem or part of a solution?

If the interviewer can determine these three things favorably, then a fourth issue is raised:

4. How much will you cost me?

Every tough question ever asked in an interview is meant to address one of these four issues.

Job hunters must understand and recognize what information is being asked for if they are to formulate appropriate responses.

THE INTERVIEWER'S CONCERNS: NUMBER ONE

Can you actually do the job? Is your experience, training, education, aptitude, and interest sufficient so you will be productive for me?

In most interviews, the majority of questions asked are to determine if you can actually do the job for which you are interviewing. If you cannot demonstrate in your answers that you can do the job, you will likely not be considered a serious candidate for the job.

Here are some tough questions often asked to elicit this information:

13. What did you like most and least in your last job?

14. Which do you prefer: words or numbers?

16. What financial responsibilities have you had?

20. Are you sure you have the qualifications for this job?

30. What interests you most about this job?

57. What do you see as the major trends in our field?

58. Why do you think you have the potential for this job?

64. How do you define the position for which you are applying?

70. How do you improve yourself professionally?

72. What can you offer us?

73. What have you achieved up to this point in your life?*

97. What are your strengths and weaknesses?*

The primary strategy for dealing with these types of questions is to provide concise and concrete information.

- Ⱥ   Answer with positive information.
- Ⱥ   Answer with facts and figures.
- Ⱥ   Answer with examples of your skills and abilities.
- Ⱥ   Answer with statistical information.
- Ⱥ   Answer by discussing your past experience.
- Ⱥ   Answer by listing your strongest skills.
- Ⱥ   Answer by detailing your accomplishments.
- Ⱥ   Answer by listing tasks you can do/have done.
- Ⱥ   Answer by outlining your knowledge.

THE INTERVIEWER'S CONCERNS: NUMBER TWO

Who are you? What are you like?
What characteristics and traits do you possess?

In addition to determining that you can do the job, the issue of who you are must be covered. No interviewer can make a decision to hire someone without having a sense of who they are as a person. It is critical information and often is considered very seriously when deciding whom to hire.

Tough questions (or statements) often asked to elicit this information include the following:

1. Talk about yourself.

18. What makes you unique?

26. What are your outside interests? How do you spend your free time?

27. What makes you angry?

38. Do you have regrets?

45. Are you a leader?*

46. What do you like to read?

49. Are you creative?

51. How do you operate under stress?

66. What are your weak points and your limitations?

73. What have you achieved up to this point in your life?*

78. Who are you?

81. What is your biggest failure?

83. Could you describe your worst day and how you dealt with it?

84. Do you have a nickname?

87. So?

88. Are you honest?

91. What type of decision do you least like to make?

96. What are your strengths and weaknesses?*

The primary strategy for dealing with these types of questions is to provide positive and truthful information about who you are.

- Answer with examples.
- Answer by listing activities and interests.
- Answer by focusing on job-related issues when appropriate.
- Answer by listing personal achievements.
- Answer by giving examples of personal growth.

A Answer with passion.

A Answer by suggesting an exchange of ideas about a job-related subject.

A Answer by quickly and briefly stating any negative information and moving to another topic immediately.

THE INTERVIEWER'S CONCERNS: NUMBER THREE

Will you fit in with the others in my company/organization? Will you be part of a problem or part of a solution?

Most employers have had bad experiences in the past when hiring people and need to know that they won't be making a mistake by hiring you. You must make the interviewer feel the risks to them are very limited if you are hired.

These are some of the tough questions often asked to elicit this information:

4. How do you react when you realize that you have made a mistake?

8. How long will you stay with us?

10. How would you describe your last boss?

12. How do you think your subordinates perceive you?

23. Have you ever worked with a difficult person?

34. Can you discuss a time you had a disagreement with your last boss?

45. Are you a leader?*

54. What is the most difficult task for the person who holds the responsibility?

60. How much time will you need before you are fully operational?

61. What is your work style?

76. Why were you fired from your last job?

90. What do you expect from us?

92. With what type of people do you have the most difficulty dealing?

98. How would you rate your last employer?

101. How would you characterize your relationships with your colleagues?

The primary strategy for dealing with this type of question is to provide information about how you have reacted in the past and to show there will be no surprises from you in the future to make the interviewer sorry he or she hired you.

- A Answer with examples.

- A Answer by showing methods you use to deal with people.

- A Answer by listing time frames.

- A Answer by using comments others have made about you.

- A Answer by discussing others only in positive terms.

- A Answer by defining terms so communication is always clear and answers are precise.

- A Answer by suggesting strategies for dealing with problems.

- A Answer by listing your interpersonal skills.

* Note that these questions (along with many others) may elicit information that can be used to address any or all three concerns an interviewer has. The way the information is interpreted and used will depend on how you respond.

THE INTERVIEWER'S CONCERNS: NUMBER FOUR

How much will you cost me?

If an interviewer can satisfactorily address the three preceding issues in an interview and is interested in you as a potential employee, the fourth issue then, and only then, becomes relevant. An interviewer will only address the cost issue seriously if you are a viable candidate for the job.

Tough questions often asked to elicit this information include the following:

2. What was your last salary?

5. Are you willing to lower your salary expectations?

17. How did you justify your salary in your last job?

31. Do you have a preference for salary based on seniority or merit?

47. At your age, why don't you earn a higher salary?

68. What are you worth?

71. What salary would you propose for this job, if you were me?

74. What salary range is acceptable to you?

94. Would you be willing to accept a salary cut of 50 percent for a training period of six months?

The primary strategy for dealing with this type of question is to delay discussion of salary until all other issues are settled satisfactorily for both the interviewer and candidate. Once that is done, the candidate must show the value of his contribution.

- Answer by postponing discussion if too early in the interview.
- Answer by redirecting the discussion to other topics.
- Answer by making the interviewer be the first to mention a specific amount.
- Answer by using ranges whenever possible.
- Answer by asking questions for clarification.
- Answer by defining terms so communication is always clear and answers are precise.
- Answer by detailing specific accomplishments to show your worth.

- Answer by listing benefits of value you will accept.
- Answer by corresponding the responsibilities of the job to value.
- Answer by discussing salary curves.

2
Formulating
Your Response

A candidate can respond in several ways to questions asked in an interview. Every question asked will elicit some information from the person being interviewed, even if the person remains silent.

Different responses can be effective and appropriate at different times and in different situations. Carefully evaluate what is the best strategy to use for certain questions, and then proceed.

The following are seven strategies for responding to questions from interviewers:

1. Provide information.

2. Rephrase the question or ask another one.

3. Answer carefully or avoid answering altogether.

4. Reassure your interviewer.

5. Use humor.

6. Control your body language.

7. Smile, relax, and look happy.

1. Provide information. If a question is straightforward and calls for specific information, remain calm and provide the information asked for in a concise fashion.

Interviewers who are good at their job want you talk most of the time so they can get sufficient information from you. Knowing this will allow you to practice your answers so you do not ramble or seem unprepared.

For example, if asked:

"What can you offer us?"

you might respond by mentioning three key tasks of the job that you can do.

2. Rephrase the question or ask another one. Some questions do not demand an answer immediately. You may need more time to reflect on the best and most appropriate answer. Additionally, interviewers often word questions vaguely to see how you will respond. When this is the case, you must get more specific details before you can answer well. It is then appropriate to ask, "Could you please be more specific?" or, "What specific areas are you curious about, my professional achievements or personal characteristics?"

For example if asked:

"Are you honest?"

you might respond, "May I know your reason for asking?"

When you rephrase the existing question or ask another question, you clarify exactly what kind of information is wanted from you.

3. Answer carefully or avoid answering altogether. For some questions, it is best to try to avoid answering altogether. If you must answer, be very careful about what you say.

Some tough questions are dangerous to answer too quickly (if at all). When faced with this type of question, try to avoid answering by using humor, or even remaining silent and then suggesting another topic to discuss before returning to the difficult question.

For example if asked:

"What are you worth?"

you might respond, "My career path is important to me, and decisions influencing its direction are not based primarily on financial concerns. Therefore, perhaps I can address this question after we have discussed my qualifications further."

4. Reassure your interviewer. For some questions, it is your job to describe achievements that will make your interviewer feel the risk in hiring you is limited. Describe one or two things you have done in the past to show what you have mastered, using examples with facts, figures, and tangible proof.

For example if asked:

"Why do you think you have the potential for this job?"

you might respond, "My three strongest qualifications for this job are … " (mention three strong points).

5. Use humor. Some questions lend themselves to humorous answers, especially when a rational answer will not reassure your interviewer. Instead, demonstrate that the question (and the underlying issue raised by it) is not a problem for you and will therefore not be a problem for your interviewer or his organization.

Although humor can be risky in an interview, and it can be challenging to apply appropriately, it is often the best tool to deal with tough questions. It is never a good idea, however, to try to use humor if you have not built some type of rapport with your interviewer. Proceed carefully and use caution!

For example if asked:

"Would you like to sit in my chair one day?"

you might respond, "Yes, if you find a chair more comfortable!"

Using humor to respond can show the interviewer that you are not knocked off balance by the question and responding in this way will likely be more impressive than any factual information you could provide.

6. Control your body language. When asked certain questions, you must be sure not to betray yourself with your non-verbal language. This is often an immediate and unconscious response. When asked a tough question that is embarrassing or difficult to answer because of an unflattering factor in the past, some people cough slightly, some blush, some look down at the floor, some wring their hands, etc. Sometimes the signs are even more subtle and less visible, such as tightening the muscles in the temples or moving the shoulders down slightly.

Interviewers are often very good at noticing these things—without letting you know they have noticed.

To prepare for these types of questions you need practice. Have a friend ask questions that cause you problems, and have them watch for any body language that might betray your true feelings. Practicing with a friend can help you master your response to these questions so you feel comfortable with them. You can also practice by looking in a mirror.

For example if asked:

"Are you willing to lower your salary expectations?"

you might respond, "By how much?" (said without showing any emotion, even if this upsets you).

7. Smile, relax, and look happy. The best approach for some questions is to take it easy—smile, relax, and look happy. Nothing is more powerful than a smile. It is even more effective when you look directly into the interviewer's eyes and are sure of yourself.

What is important is how you look on the outside, and not what you feel (you may be scared or paralyzed inside). You can master this technique by training, just as you do for controlling your body language. Look at your smile in the mirror. Avoid a fake expression and be sincere.

For example if asked:

"How do you rate my style of conducting this interview?"

you might respond by waiting a few seconds, smiling, and saying, "I liked it."

Convince yourself there is no question you would rather answer, and give the interviewer a big smile! It is difficult for an interviewer to remain neutral about someone who is both enthusiastic and spontaneous.

Conclusion

Balance the above strategies when interviewing. You do not want to use humor too much and be considered overconfident. By the same token, if you never smile or relax, you will likely be deemed too serious or nervous. You may also find it appropriate to combine certain strategies like rephrasing a question and then providing information. By becoming familiar with the questions you will be asked, you can perfect the best way to respond and can interview with full confidence that you are prepared to do your best.

You will be successful with your preparation when you attend an interview and are not asked a single question for which you have not previously prepared a good response.

101 Toughest
Interview Questions

. . . and Answers
that Win the Job!

Talk about yourself!

Talk about yourself!

(Ask one of the following to get a better
idea of what the interviewer wants.
Then develop your response
in less than two minutes.)

A **Certainly. What specific point would you like me to discuss further?**

A **With pleasure! Something from my past or a recent achievement?**

A **What would you like to talk about, a professional or personal issue?**

A **With pleasure! Should I develop something in detail or just give you a brief summary?**

What was
your last salary?

What was your last salary?

A **My last salary was exactly within the range that I now seek, which is between _____ and _____ (mention a range).**

A **My last employer and I had an agreement that forbids me from discussing my salary, either within the company or outside.**

A **I will gladly discuss my last salary, after we have negotiated my future salary.**

A **My salary was completely consistent with the contribution I made to my last employer.**

Have you ever laid off or fired a person?

Have you ever laid off or fired a person?

A **No.**

A **Yes. It is a difficult task, so I always did my best to be tactful and compassionate.**

A **Yes, several times. I took full responsibility in my job for everything. I believe I handled it correctly.**

A **Yes. It is part of a supervisor's job, and you must be ready to do it.**

A **Yes, though it was difficult, I believe it is important for everyone's morale to have only highly competent people on staff.**

How do you react when you realize that you have made a mistake?

How do you react when you realize that you have made a mistake?

A I study the consequences and then react.

A I pause to analyze the situation and then take corrective steps.

A I assume my responsibility and get back to work again.

A I ask for the opinions and advice of friends and co-workers.

A I discuss the situation with my supervisor and develop a strategy so I don't repeat my mistake.

Are you willing to lower your salary expectations?

Are you willing to lower your salary expectations?

A Yes. (Remain quiet.)

A Yes, if you readjust the salary after an initial period that we negotiate now.

A Yes, if we can readdress it later to be commensurate with the responsibilities entrusted to me.

A What you call "salary expectations" is the just compensation for my work. However, I remain open to discussion.

A Yes, if it's possible to be compensated with other nonsalary benefits.

A If the work environment is good and there are strong possibilities for promotion, I would consider it.

A It depends on the job description.

A By how much?

Should I make you a firm job offer?

Should I make you a firm job offer?

A Yes, after having specified to me ... (name it).

A I would appreciate it very much!

A Yes, because my skills match your requirements and I am very interested in the job.

A Yes, I have always had a keen interest and desire for these kinds of responsibilities.

A I would prefer we discuss the job requirements in greater depth before an offer is made.

Why are you looking for a job?

Why are you looking for a job?

A I am not looking for a job. I am offering my services to you.

A My present job no longer matches my aspirations and goals.

A I am making a career change and wish to offer my services to a corporation that . . . (give one or two distinctive features).

A I have reevaluated my goals and am starting a new phase in my career.

How long will you stay with us?

How long will you stay with us?

A As long as I can contribute to your development.

A I am looking for a long-term position.

A I am a very loyal person.

A As long as the organization continues to grow.

A As long as it is a mutually satisfying relationship.

Why have you been unemployed for so long?

Why have you been unemployed for so long?

A It took time to polish my knowledge in _____ (name the topic, i.e., computers or foreign languages).

A I took time to do a thorough self-assessment. Now everything is clear. The proof . . . I am in your office!

A I carefully study the proposals made to me and consider only those options that will provide me with quality work.

A I will only accept a job that fits my qualifications.

How would you describe your last boss?

How would you describe your last boss?

A **A very competent person who knows her job.**

A **A person who has excellent relationships with his subordinates and people in general.**

A **A very efficient person who is well organized and with whom I loved working.**

A **An excellent specialist in the field.**

A **Due to the nature of my job, we had limited contact. Our relationship was satisfactory but not overly personal.**

Please discuss a decision you made that was questioned.

Please discuss a decision you made that was questioned.

A Certainly. When I decided to leave my job in _____, my boss tried to persuade me I was wrong to leave.

A Friends tried to persuade me not to study _____ (name the subject). However, I am glad I did.

A Although I tried to explain my decision to my boss when we disagreed, I realized I did not incorporate two important strategic elements in my decision. I recognized my presentation was not as thorough as it should have been.

How do you think your subordinates perceive you?

How do you think your subordinates perceive you?

A They perceive me as someone who is demanding, but fair and open to discussion.

A They like me, I think.

A I am a very easy person to get along with and my skills as a mediator are well known.

A In the last two years turnover has decreased and no employees have left.

What did you like most and least in your last job?

What did you like most and least in your last job?

A (Mention what you liked best and do not say anything about what you liked least.)

A What I liked most were the challenges I found there. (Change the subject.)

A The least . . . The most . . .
(Finish with something positive).

A The least . . . like everyone else, routine work. The most . . . (mention something of value).

A The most . . . creativity.

A The least . . . repetitive tasks, which are unfortunately necessary to keep things running smoothly.

Which do you prefer: numbers or words?

Which do you prefer: numbers or words?

A **Both: in the context of research the use of numbers is quite familiar to me. In developing a theory, I like writing.**

A **Words. It is easier to sell a vacation on the destination than it is on the taxes!**

A **Numbers. It is always easier to develop a rationale based on numbers than on theories.**

A **My background and experience have provided me with a stronger faculty for numbers than for words.**

A **I feel very comfortable with numbers; however, I find words more challenging and interesting.**

How many people did you supervise at any given time?

How many people did you supervise at any given time?

A I have not had the chance to supervise others yet, but I am fully prepared to do so.

A Between _____ and _____ , depending on the size of the project.

A Outside of work, I am often in charge of many people. (Give an example.)

A I have had experience supervising small administrative and production teams.

A There were/are _____ people under my supervision at my last/present job.

What financial responsibilities have you had?

What financial responsibilities have you had?

A Since the age of sixteen, I have planned my own budget.

A I had technical responsibilities that translated into financial responsibilities.

A I plan the budget for my family.

A I managed to multiply sales threefold in an eight-month period.

How did you justify your salary in your last job?

How did you justify your salary in your last job?

A I replaced two people for a period of two years in the largest department.

A I decreased turnover by _____ percent.

A Very simply, I was paid by volume of production . . . or on a commission basis.

A My objectives were very clear, and I often worked overtime to meet them.

A By ensuring that over 50 percent of the customer base remained loyal to the organization.

A I took my responsibilities seriously to make sure nothing went wrong (for example, production never had to be stopped).

A I did my job with heart and I succeeded in . . . (mention one or two achievements).

A By generating a contribution that was five times the size of my salary.

What makes you unique?

What makes you unique?

A Three things: a sound basic technical background, additional training in management, and international experience.

A Unique things should be in museums. I am mostly practical.

A A different approach from most . . . (give one or two examples).

A I think I am ideally suited for the job and I like it very much.

What are the things that bore you the most?

What are the things that bore you the most?

A To have to do the same thing over and over.

A Inflexible and narrow-minded people.

A To stay in one place and do nothing; to have the feeling I am not progressing.

Are you sure you have the qualifications for this job?

Are you sure you have the qualifications for this job?

A Are you testing me?

A This job is exactly what I want to do, and I have carefully checked to be sure that I have the potential and skills for it.

A Test me.

Have you heard any criticism of our organization?

Have you heard any criticism of our organization?

A I learned that you are very demanding with your employees. I must admit that this does not bother me; on the contrary, I respect it.

A The obsession that your company has with self-promotion in the media.

A Comments are usually very positive.

A That you are not the market leader in this field.

How do you respond when your ideas are rejected?

How do you respond when your ideas are rejected?

A I suggest other possibilities.

A I negotiate a compromise.

A I modify them and use another avenue to try again.

A I try to understand the reason and readjust my sales pitch.

A I use the opportunity to question myself.

A I stand firm if I am convinced I am right.

A I keep the key components of my proposal and I modify the rest.

Have you ever worked
with a difficult person?

Have you ever worked
with a difficult person?

A Yes. It stimulates me.

A Complex people, yes. Difficult, I don't think so.

A Yes, several times. It is then very important to clarify objectives and responsibilities.

A Not yet. I don't think I attract them, or I just don't perceive them that way.

Have you had financial difficulties in the past?

Have you had financial difficulties in the past?

A **Like everyone, I have. I now have a budget.**

A **Yes, at one time. I managed to overcome them and I learned to always have a plan B.**

A **Not yet. I have always been very careful.**

A **Yes. When I bought a house, I had five difficult years, but happily they are in the past.**

What is your opinion on the importance of academic degrees?

What is your opinion on the importance of academic degrees?

A They are excellent when matched with professional experience.

A Necessary, but not sufficient.

A I prefer to be judged by my work achievements and my personality.

A Human qualities (like personality traits and skills) are as important as education.

What are your outside interests? How do you spend your free time?

What are your outside interests? How do you spend your free time?

A (**Mention sports or cultural activities you enjoy. However, if you participate in an extracurricular activity that might be seen negatively by the employer, do not discuss it.**)

A I use my free time for reading.

A I pursue activities different from my work. (I make pottery, I listen to music, etc.)

A I use my leisure time to exercise so that I can maintain my stamina for my work.

A I train and enrich my mind through conferences and reading.

What makes you angry?

What makes you angry?

A Lies.

A When I am not included in a project for which I think I have the ability or knowledge.

A Injustice.

A People whose passivity and lack of effort contribute to the downfall of a company.

Would you like to sit in my chair one day?

Would you like to sit in my chair one day?

A **Of course.**

A **Yes, when my level of efficiency matches yours.**

A **My wish, in terms of a mid-range goal, is to be in a job where the responsibilities are similar to the ones you have.**

A **Yes, as soon as you have been promoted.**

A **Not for the time being; maybe one day.**

A **Yes, if you find a chair more comfortable!**

A **Could I try it right now?**

Silence.

Silence.
(It is one way of interviewing.)

A (Count on your fingers under the table. Usually the interviewer will resume talking before you reach five!)

A (Ask a question that radically changes the subject and brings the conversation back to a point your interviewer seems interested in discussing.)

A (Ask a question about the organization.)

A (Ask for additional information.)

A (Remain silent, and after five to seven seconds say, "Did I answer your silence?")

A Could we summarize what we have just covered in the last ten minutes?

A If we have covered everything, which of us will initiate the next contact?

A Do you have any other questions?

What interests you most about this job?

What interests you most about this job?

A I like this job because it uses both my enthusiasm and knowledge.

A This job is the logical continuation of the past seven years I have spent as a . . . (mention a title or activity).

A This job interests me because of the tasks involved; your company interests me because of its strategy and values.

A This job corresponds to what I have been interested in for a long time: a good balance between short- and long-term activities.

Do you have a preference for salary based on seniority or merit?

Do you have a preference for salary based on seniority or merit?

A I don't see the relationship between your question and the job to be filled.

A I think your question is relevant. Would you object if I answered it a little bit later?

A May I ask you to elaborate on two or three characteristics of your salary policy?

A How does internal promotion actually occur in your company?

Where do you see yourself on a long-term basis?

Where do you see yourself on a long-term basis?

A In a job where I can maximize profitability for your organization.

A By "long term," do you mean five years or fifteen years?

A For me, this job is my short-term goal and a career with your company is my long-term goal.

A Where I am efficient and can thrive and develop.

A Continuing to work in a job that brings me joy and makes a difference to others.

What problems
do you have?

What problems do you have?

 Soon I will have to choose between two firm job offers.

 What type of problems? Professional, personal, or family?

 Everything is fine. Thank you for asking. (Smile!)

Can you discuss a time you had a disagreement with your last boss?

Can you discuss a time you had a disagreement with your last boss?

A We have had discussions about strategic standpoints; however, we always ended up in agreement.

A We never had one.

A We don't like the same movies.

A We had two different alternatives to solve a problem. We chose neither alternative and, instead, agreed on a third one.

What has been the most difficult decision you have had to make in the last 12 months?

What has been the most difficult decision you have had to make in the last 12 months?

A (Mention a decision and show how you managed to solve the problem.)

A There is no such thing as a difficult decision when you have thoroughly analyzed the situation.

A For me, when decisions present themselves, I have no problem taking responsibility.

A Turning down a job that paid very well but did not interest me very much.

A A very personal decision, but I was able to settle it.

A How best to approach you to set up this interview!

Which of your achievements gave you the greatest satisfaction?

Which of your achievements gave you the greatest satisfaction?

A When I was able to double our productivity and reduce our costs by 40 percent.

A I managed to succeed when everyone else thought it was impossible.

A Bringing up my children to be balanced and happy.

A To have successfully implemented a project similar to the one you now need to undertake.

How do you react when you are asked to radically change your methodology?

How do you react when you are asked to radically change your methodology?

A **I obey but still retain my autonomy.**

A **I am usually very adaptive, and I like it.**

A **At the beginning it may seem difficult, but in fact, it is stimulating and I seize the opportunity to improve my skills.**

A **I accept it after negotiating a time to carry out the tasks.**

A **I ask why; if a better outcome can be demonstrated, I accept it.**

Do you have regrets?

Do you have regrets?

A **Regrets, no. Memories, yes.**

A **Yes. I wish I had applied for this job earlier.**

A **No. I have always considered the positive side of my professional experiences.**

A **Yes. I regret not being able to use all of my creative potential in some of my past jobs.**

A **I am one of those people who only looks forward.**

A **Regrets, no. Experience, yes!**

A **Yes. (Mention one.)**

Do you think you are underqualified for this job?

Do you think you are underqualified for this job?

A I think I have the potential for the job because . . . (list two reasons).

A I am ready to attend an intensive, continuing education program for this purpose.

A For two aspects of the job, perhaps. However, I have three positive things to offer you. (Mention three qualities or achievements.)

A Are you speaking of a specific skill?

A I think I have the skills and enthusiasm necessary for this job.

A Perhaps I can elaborate on my experience in the field of _____ (name it).

I now have three candidates (including you). What criteria should I use to select the one to fill the job?

I now have three candidates (including you). What criteria should I use to select the one to fill the job?

A I love this job; I think you should select me.

A Could you describe the two other candidates?

A What are the two or three key criteria you feel are most important in your decision?

A If your three criteria are competency, enthusiasm, and perseverance, then I am the person for the job.

Don't you trust us?

Don't you trust us?

(This question is usually raised when asking for a written commitment after a promise has been made to you.)

A **I only wish to formalize the agreement we have just made.**

A **Yes, of course. I am only suggesting that we summarize, in writing, the key points of our interview.**

A **For professional reasons only, it is important to me to write down the key information.**

Why should I hire you instead of another candidate?

Why should I hire you instead of another candidate?

A I would like to have this job very much.

A After this interview, when you know me better, I am sure you will be able to answer this question yourself.

A I believe I have a lot to offer. (Summarize qualifications.)

What are the two things you most want to improve in the next several years?

What are the two things you most want to improve in the next several years?

A The performance of my subordinates and myself.

A My capacity to anticipate more rapidly the needs of the market for_____ (name it).

A My swing and my handicap. Do you play golf?

A Are you speaking in terms of my transferable skills, knowledge, or personality traits?

A Increase your market share and retain your key customers.

A The two concerns about your organization that you mentioned. (List them.)

Have you had any other firm job offers?

Have you had any other firm job offers?

A Yes.

A Yes, and I must say that I am most interested in your company.

A I am in the final process of negotiations with two other organizations.

A I have just begun my job search and things look promising. The proof is that I am in your office!

Are you a leader?

Are you a leader?

A If being listened to and respected by my subordinates means being a leader, then I am one.

A A leader, maybe. A dictator, certainly not.

A I think I have always been a leader; in groups, I have always taken leadership roles.

A If by leader you mean allowing people to reach their objectives, then I am a leader.

What do you like to read?

What do you like to read?

A Daily newspapers and historical books.

A Mostly technical magazines.

A I love daily newspapers and biographies.

A I rarely read tabloids or "fluff" literature.

At your age, why don't you earn a higher salary?

At your age, why don't you earn a higher salary?

A **My last/present job description is radically different from the one we are now discussing.**

A **Money has never been my primary motivation in a job.**

A **My previous salary did not reflect all of my additional benefits ("perks"), which had significant value.**

A **I am choosing to do what I want to do. I am not forced to work for money only.**

Would you be willing to undergo psychological testing?

Would you be willing to undergo psychological testing?

A Yes. **Could you just let me know how important these tests are in your decision-making process?**

A Yes, with pleasure, **once we know each other better.**

A Certainly. **I would only ask to know the conclusions from the testing, as is customary, I believe.**

A I prefer not to undergo tests, but offer **you as an alternative an in-depth interview so you can evaluate my personality as precisely as any test.**

A I would prefer that you judge me on **my professional achievements, and I am ready to answer any questions you have.**

Are you creative?

Are you creative?

A Could you allow me to cite a very specific example and then judge me on my results? (Name one.)

A Yes, it is one of my three main characteristics.

A I think so. In my last/present job, I . . . and . . . (mention two achievements highlighting your creativity).

A What do you mean by creative?

In your last job did you discover a problem that your predecessors had left untreated?

In your last job did you discover a problem that your predecessors had left untreated?

A Honestly, I don't know. I have had to manage by myself and I can't say that any particular problem was attributable to my predecessor(s).

A Yes. A problem that helped me develop a new technique.

A Yes, a safety practice that was not being implemented.

A No. I found my predecessor to be an extremely capable and thorough person. I was able to build on the solid foundation left to me.

How do you operate under stress?

How do you operate under stress?

A It stimulates me and makes me more efficient.

A I work just as well.

A Generally, I organize myself so that I am not under stress. If it still occurs, I manage it.

A I like objectives to be defined and have no difficulty dealing with delays. Therefore, I manage to eliminate most causes of stress.

What type of job is best suited to you, staff or management?

What type of job is best suited to you, staff or management?

A For me, these two are often be found in the same job and don't oppose each other.

A I am looking for a very diverse job. Would it be management or staff?

A In my last job, I wore a two hats, management and staff. I was adept at both.

A I have had both staff and management jobs. I feel comfortable in both of them.

A I can adapt in either case.

A I operate well in the two situations. I have a preference for . . . (mention one).

A Management when given the choice.

How did you overcome the negative impact of losing a job?

How did you overcome the negative impact of losing a job?

A **I persevered and now I have recovered.**

A **It is a good school for improving your courage.**

A **I used this period to improve my knowledge in the field of _____ (name it).**

A **I have recovered and have just launched my job-hunting campaign.**

A **I imposed a very strict routine and a full schedule upon myself.**

What is the most difficult task for the person who holds the responsibility?

What is the most difficult task for the person who holds the responsibility?

A It is not being able to share the responsibility and having to make difficult decisions alone.

A To be obliged to fire people sometimes.

A To find relevant strategies to avoid having to terminate personnel.

A Knowing how to wait for something to happen.

If you were me, what would you expect from the candidates?

If you were me, what would you expect from the candidates?

A Above all, authenticity and honesty.

A A strong personality and good self-management skills.

A The ability to do well at . . . (name a few skills or tasks), proven by a strong track record.

A Enthusiasm, competence, and perseverance.

The interview is over.
Do you have any questions
to ask me?

The interview is over.
Do you have any questions
to ask me?

A **Thank you. I think that we have covered everything.**

A **Yes, but perhaps we could discuss my questions during the next interview?**

A **Yes. What positive conclusion have you come to after this interview?**

A **Everything has been covered as far as I'm concerned. Who should take the initiative for the next contact?**

A **Yes. Could you tell me a little about yourself and how long you have been here?**

What do you see as the major trends in our field?

What do you see as the major trends in our field?

A I made a survey prior to meeting with you and I see two points. (Mention them.)

A I have one or two ideas that I need to reflect upon more before discussing.

A It is moving in the right direction. This is why I want to work in this field.

A Like many other fields: cutting costs, increasing quality, and consolidating services to the customer.

Why do you think you have the potential for this job?

Why do you think you have the potential for this job?

I know my potential and I can tell you that I plan to improve the company in two areas. (Mention two areas you are 100 percent sure you can improve.)

Two things make me believe that I can answer positively. (Mention two examples or facts as proof.)

My three strongest qualifications for this job are . . . (mention three strong points).

On the basis of your information, I think I have the potential as well as the enthusiasm and persistence that you would expect from someone working for you.

Do you think you are overqualified for this job?

Do you think you are overqualified for this job?

A What do you mean by overqualified?

A When I consider the projects for which I have been responsible, I see that I am a good match for the job.

A I feel I have many positive things I can offer your organization?

A For this job, experience is as important as qualifications.

A Which one of my degrees, diplomas, or certificates should I burn?

A What makes you believe I am over-qualified?

A Is it my résumé that gives you this impression?

A I have confidence that I can perform the tasks required in this job.

How much time will you need before you are fully operational?

How much time will you need before you are fully operational?

A To be your _____ (mention the job title)? Immediately.

A Before I can answer you, I would like to ask you two questions. (Ask them.)

A The time needed to thoroughly study the files.

A I usually adapt myself fairly quickly: Let's assume between _____ and _____ weeks.

A For the daily work, immediately. For more specific issues, the time needed to learn more about the files, your company, and your customers.

What is your work style?

What is your work style?

A **A positive style, of course!**

A **The one that is most appropriate for the situation.**

A **I am usually considered . . . (mention three qualities).**

A **I am usually very efficient in two situations: as a member of a team and working under stress.**

A **Do you want to know my style of interacting with others or my way of approaching a problem?**

A **I am not impressed by "gurus" and do not belong to any specific school of thought.**

Why are you looking for this type of job?

Why are you looking for this type of job?

A In this type of job, I can give the best of myself.

A For three reasons: diversity of tasks, freedom to organize myself personally, and the opportunity to do things methodically.

A Because my experience in this field could be highly profitable to your organization.

Why do you want to work for us?

Why do you want to work for us?

A The job to be filled and the mission to be carried out match my objectives exactly.

A Your company is known for quality work.

A I have had the experience of being in situations similar to those you face here.

A You are a company that I could offer . . . (describe three contributions).

A Your company attracts me tremendously.

A Your development projects are in line with my ambitions.

A Knowing your market, I think I would be an asset to your company.

How do you define the position for which you are applying?

How do you define the position for which you are applying?

A (List the key tasks that are critical.)

A A job where one has to . . . (list three skills and one or two difficult working conditions).

A A job where one has to be very discreet and always available.

A A difficult job with challenges to seize and demanding customers.

A A job I would adore.

What attracts you most about this job?

What attracts you most about this job?

A Contact with customers.

A The opportunity to use my skills.

A The dynamic nature of your company and the objectives of the job.

A The scope of my responsibilities.

What are your weak points and your limitations?

What are your weak points and your limitations?

A I used to be overly meticulous, but I am now more efficient.

A My weak point is sometimes being unaware of my limits.

A I sometimes have too much passion for things I undertake.

A I am very curious.

A I used to have a particular weak point; however, over the last five years I have worked hard to overcome it.

What are your future ambitions?

What are your future ambitions?

A My ambition is to develop social integration techniques, and this job matches exactly what I seek.

A I want to develop my career.

A To work in a job that allows me to thrive and develop my potential while furthering the interest of the organization.

A To satisfy your customers.

What are you worth?

What are you worth?

A If you think that I am the person for the job, what is your proposal?

A My career path is important to me, and decisions influencing its direction are not based primarily on financial concerns. Therefore, perhaps I can address this question after we have discussed my qualifications further.

A Thank you for bringing this up; before we discuss this, could you please elaborate on the following job responsibilities? (Name them.)

A This depends upon the responsibilities of the job.

What do you know about us?

What do you know about us?

A (Mention three things that you really appreciate about their products or services.)

A (Describe their public image.)

A I know that you have . . . (mention two or three specific facts about the company's recent performance).

A I visited your company previously; I am returning as a candidate, because I liked the feeling here.

A The good reputation of your company and the quality of your products/services.

How do you improve yourself professionally?

How do you improve yourself professionally?

A **In three ways: I read and study professional magazines, attend conferences, and take appropriate continuing education courses.**

A **I always attend continuing education classes, since I am a self-made person.**

A **I teach courses and give speeches.**

A **I am always aware of technical break-throughs and study them to be enriched professionally.**

A **I risk failure by trying new things, so that I may develop new skills and interests.**

What salary would you propose for this job, if you were me?

What salary would you propose for this job, if you were me?

A A salary that corresponds to the job and its responsibilities.

A I like your question. For me, salary is not a key factor.

A A salary that matches other salaries in your company will fit me.

A I know if we agree on the job, we will agree on the salary.

What can you offer us?

What can you offer us?

A (Mention three qualities.)

A (Mention three key tasks of the job that you can do.)

A A good knowledge of your competition, as I have been working in this field.

What have you achieved up to this point in your life?

What have you achieved up to this point in your life?

A (Mention three points, i.e., launching products X, Y, and Z; reorganizing a division; quality control of A, B, and C.) Would you like me to develop one of these points in more detail?

A (Mention several very specific examples.)

A Being a very social person I always strive to improve relationships between people in the organizations for which I've worked.

A Increasing of gains, decreasing of costs and avoiding errors. Do you want examples?

A Three wonderful children! Are you a parent as well?

A In which field, professional or personal?

A It's rather long to tell. Here are my three key achievements. (Name three.)

What salary range is acceptable to you?

What salary range is acceptable to you?

A I wish to earn a salary that is commensurate with my potential and future contribution.

A I wish to make between _____ and _____ within three to five years.

A I am interested in the range of _____ and _____ , which we can narrow down once I have more information on the job to be filled.

A Your question is interesting. For me, the key issue is to know each other well first.

A What I want from a job is more important than what I want in a salary.

A I would appreciate, at this stage, to have more information on the job, so I can fairly measure my impact on the profitability of your department/division/company.

Why did you quit your last job?

Why did you quit your last job?

A **My professional knowledge was not used. I want to use it in your field.**

A **I have always worked in very stimulating situations where I had to commit myself. I realized this would not be the case in the next two or three years if I remained there.**

A **For strategic and budgetary reasons, my division is being eliminated.**

A **I have just received from my employer a promotion that does not match what I want: They offered me a staff position, and believe I am better suited for a management position.**

Why were you fired from your last job?

Why were you fired from your last job?

A The project for which I was responsible was completed. I saw it to the end.

A The division to which I belonged was completely eliminated.

A I turned down a proposal for which my skills would not have been used profitably.

A My employer believed my experience would allow me to find a job more easily than other members of the organization. The proof is that I am in your office!

A My employer has not been able to offer me a job matching my professional objectives.

A My division was moved.

A I was not doing some of the things I needed to do. I took responsibility for this and am much improved.

What do you desire most in your next job?

What do you desire most in your next job?

A (Show your decisiveness and your commitment.)

A (Take one of the top three tasks for the job, given to you by them, and elaborate on it.)

A (Answer quickly and decisively; then change the subject.)

A To become responsible and contribute.

A The pleasure to express myself.

A That you are satisfied with me.

A Team work in which the possibility for me to take individual initiative exists.

Who are you?

Who are you?

A (Manage not to answer. Try to talk instead about a theme you want to develop.)

A I work in a field very close to . . . (mention the reason for your interest in them).

A I came to exchange ideas with you about _____, something your company is involved in that interests me greatly.

A I am passionate about . . . (mention the reason for your interest in them).

A I am at a crossroads and one project I am considering is . . . (mention the project). I would like to have your point of view on it.

If you were conducting this interview, what would you do differently?

If you were conducting this interview, what would you do differently?

A I really love the sound of this job and I, like you, would make it a point to find the right person.

A I would probably do it differently because we are different. However, I must say I appreciate your style.

A I might have discussed additional characteristics such as availability, sense of humor, etc.

A How can I answer that? I appreciate your professionalism.

How do you rate my style of conducting this interview?

How do you rate my style of conducting this interview?

A (Summarize three key points of the interview and confirm your interest.)

A (Wait a few seconds, smile, and say, "Good," or "I liked it.")

A Very informative and very friendly.

A Very good. For me, the job description is clear and attractive, and you gave me enough time to express myself as well.

A Excellent! I think you can now decide. (Smile and remain silent.)

A I thank you very much and I appreciate our exchange. How do we follow up?

What is your
biggest failure?

What is your biggest failure?

A (Three pieces of advice: never use the word *failure*, limit your answer to less than twenty seconds, and once answered, ask a question quickly to change the subject.)

A It was in a nonprofessional area, and has helped me develop persistence.

A I always have a plan **B** for anything I undertake, therefore I always have more than one way to react.

A Your question comes a little early in my career.

A I don't really remember a specific example. I try to learn from my experiences.

Of the job offers you have received (including ours), how will you decide which you will accept?

Of the job offers you have received (including ours), how will you decide which you will accept?

A **Yours, with enthusiasm.**

A **Of the three, I rank yours first.**

A **My decision is already 90 percent in your favor. Please give me forty-eight hours to confirm it.**

A **In your organization, two points are very positive (_____ and _____). Please give me forty-eight hours to confirm my decision.**

Could you describe your worst day and how you dealt with it?

Could you describe your worst day and how you dealt with it?

A (Mention one funny example that has nothing to do with the job or a drama that was personal in nature.)

A From a professional or personal stand-point?

A Are you married?!

A I only remember good days.

A When I met a movie star I admired, and I was tongue-tied!

A When? Three months ago, three years ago, or ten years ago?

Do you have a nickname?

Do you have a nickname?

A Yes, . . . (mention it).

A No, not as far as I know!

A My name is easy to remember. Therefore, I have no nickname.

A I don't have one. Do you like giving nick-names?

A My friends call me _____.

If I were to make you a firm job offer, what would your answer be?

If I were to make you a firm job offer, what would your answer be?

A I would be delighted to discuss that; beforehand, however, would you please elaborate on the following points . . . (name them)?

A I would ask you for some time to reflect.

A I would be delighted, and I think we would have no problem agreeing on the specifics.

A Thank you very much for your trust. I believe you will be happy to have me working for you.

How would you describe your ideal working conditions?

How would you describe your ideal working conditions?

A (Mention two or three.)

A What do you mean by ideal?

A Do you want my point of view on very specific working conditions or just an overview?

A May we discuss the job description before I answer you?

So?

So?

(Opening—careful and polite)

A May I be seated?

A Thank you for seeing me and offering me ten minutes of your time.

(Opening—minor initiative)

A Where would you like to begin?

A Would you like me to talk about myself or would you rather give me some details about the job?

(Opening—major initiative)

A The reason I have approached you is ... (give the reason). In this context, may I ask you for more details about your organization?

A Thank you for the interview. Could we start by clarifying two tasks in your job description? The first one ... (name it).

A Before we begin, may I ask you which specific point in my letter made you decide to ask me in for an interview?

Are you honest?

Are you honest?

A I always give the best of myself.

A I believe it is one of my three strongest traits.

A May I know the reason you ask this?

A Your questions is extremely straightfor- ward, and I do not mind. I am an honest person.

Are you looking for a limited or unlimited time contract?

Are you looking for a limited or unlimited time contract?

Ⓐ **What can you offer?**

Ⓐ **A limited-time contract would suit me best.**

Ⓐ **A full-time contract would suit me best.**

Ⓐ **Before we discuss the details of a contract, could we please clarify the responsibilities of the job?**

Ⓐ **I am most attracted by an interesting job. The time frame for any contract is of secondary concern.**

Ⓐ **I am undecided about which type of relationship I would like. I am open to any possibility.**

What do you expect from us?

What do you expect from us?

Ⓐ The chance to prove my enthusiasm and efficiency.

Ⓐ A firm job offer.

Ⓐ A fair exchange; to give a lot and receive a lot.

Ⓐ To be allowed to use my competency in this field.

Ⓐ The compensation for what I give to you.

What type of decision do you least like to make?

What type of decision do you least like to make?

A When filling a job opening, having to choose between two persons who are both enthusiastic and competent.

A I do not like to say no; sometimes it is essential for efficiency, however.

A In what respect? Professionally or personally?

A A strategic decision involving top management.

With what type of people do you have the most difficulty dealing?

With what type of people do you have the most difficulty dealing?

A I am flexible and adapt to most people. However, stubborn people do not inspire me.

A Misunderstanding comes from bad communication, so I make it a point to keep people around me informed.

A I prefer to work with people who are open and honest, even when a situation is difficult.

A I make it a point to clear up any source of misunderstanding, which makes it easy to deal with anyone.

Are your past actions consistent with your values?

Are your past actions consistent with your values?

A Yes. I am true to myself and others.

A Yes. I have peace of mind and sleep well.

A My future is on the same track as my past.

A Oh, yes! Positively.

Would you be willing to accept a salary cut of 50 percent for a training period of six months?

Would you be willing to accept a salary cut of 50 percent for a training period of six months?

A Could you describe the training?

A Do you make this type of proposal to all the candidates?

A The idea of improving myself and learning new techniques interests me a lot. Could you please describe this training?

A I am very interested in this job. Could we discuss this point later?

A What responsibilities would I have after this training period?

What made you decide to write us?

What made you decide to write us?

A **(Mention one recent achievement or positive characteristic of the company.)**

A **(Reiterate what you wrote in your application letter.)**

A **I decided to offer my services to a company in your field. I have approached three organizations, yours among them.**

A **The reputation of your company.**

A **Several people I spoke with suggested I contact you.**

What are your strengths and weaknesses?

What are your strengths and weaknesses?

A (Take less than one minute to answer; then change the subject.)

A (Limit yourself to mentioning three strong points and say "I have the weaknesses of my strengths"; then change the subject.)

A (Mention three strong points, three weak points, one strong point; then change the subject.)

A I would rather tell you my three key characteristics (mention three strong points).

A I am rather persistent; when I set an objective, I do not stop until I have reached it.

A Rather than mentioning my weaknesses and strengths, may I tell you of two achievements that reveal a lot about my character?

Have you approached other organizations?

Have you approached other organizations?

A I was doing a similar job in a field related to yours.

A This job offers me exactly what I want to do. Another company cannot offer me this.

A Yes.

A Yes, two as of now.

A Yes: company **ABC** and company **XYZ**.

How would you rate your last employer?

How would you rate your last employer?

A My last employer was very professional.

A We parted on good terms. I had a limited-time contract with them.

A My last employer was nice and efficient. I loved working with them.

A I continue to have an excellent personal and professional relationship with them.

A From which standpoint? Personal or professional?

How would you respond if I told you that your performance has not been very good?

How would you respond if I told you that your performance has not been very good?

A **Is that a conclusion or a trick question?**

A **Did you identify a weakness in my attitude or in the way I express myself?**

A **May I ask you to elaborate?**

A **I would say I need to improve. However, this in no way lessens the interest I have in this job.**

A **Please elaborate on the points I need to improve so I may learn from you.**

A **I think I am the right candidate for this job. The challenge is important and I am a little nervous.**

What is the status of your job hunt?

What is the status of your job hunt?

(At the beginning of your job hunt)

A I am optimistic. The first phase has been to set up and gather information in order to be more efficient. I have just launched the second phase: approaching organizations.

(In an advanced negotiation process)

A I am doing fine. I have established contacts with four companies (including yours). Negotiations are progressing with two of them.

(If you have firm job offers)

A I am doing fine. I have received two firm proposals from companies. I soon will face the difficult decision of which to choose.

How would you characterize your relationships with your colleagues?

How would you characterize your relationships with your colleagues?

A **Excellent. In the type of work I do, I could not operate without their support and confidence.**

A **I have excellent relationships with them; there is harmony and sympathy for one another.**

A **Frank and warm.**

A **I have always had excellent relationships, and I have been fortunate to be part of egalitarian teams.**

A **The nature of my work was generally solitary, so my colleagues were my boss, my customers, and my suppliers. My relationships were loyal, honest, and warm.**

About the Authors

A leading pioneer for over 25 years in career design and job hunting, **Daniel Porot** is an internationally recognized career expert. Daniel received his MBA in 1966 from the Business School of France, Insead, and began his career with Exxon and Amoco before starting his own business in 1971.

He has authored more than a dozen best-selling French-language career books, translated Richard N. Bolles's *What Color is Your Parachute?* into French, and written *The Pie Method for Career Success,* his first book for U.S. audiences.

In addition, he has personally trained more than 11,000 job hunters and 600 career counselors, and his training materials have been used by over one million job hunters worldwide. For the last eighteen years, Daniel has also taught an annual two-week workshop with Richard Bolles.

He lives in Geneva, Switzerland, with his wife and four children.

 **Frances Bolles Haynes** has worked in the field of career development for over twenty years. She began her career in Phoenix, helping CETA participants find employment. She then moved to Jackson, Mississippi, where she set up a successful job-hunting program based on the Job Club model, pioneered by Nathan Azrin.

She has worked with Daniel Porot for many years, and has served on the training staff of Richard Bolles. She is thankful to them both for their wisdom and genius.

Frances lives in Newport Beach, California, with her husband, Peter, and son, Donald.